JOHANN SEBASTIAN BACH

Air from Suite No. 3 in D

'Air on the G string'

Arranged for Violin and Piano by
Für Violine und Klavier bearbeitet von
Arthur Campbell

EIGENTUM DES VERLEGERS · ALLE RECHTE VORBEHALTEN
ALL RIGHTS RESERVED

EDITION PETERS

London · Frankfurt/M. · Leipzig · New York

Air from Suite No. 3 in D
'Air on the G string'

J. S. Bach
arr. Arthur Campbell

Edition Peters No. 7355
© Copyright 1992 by Hinrichsen Edition, Peters Edition Ltd., London

JOHANN SEBASTIAN BACH

Air from Suite No. 3 in D

'Air on the G string'

Arranged for Violin and Piano by
Für Violine und Klavier bearbeitet von
Arthur Campbell

Violin

EIGENTUM DES VERLEGERS · ALLE RECHTE VORBEHALTEN
ALL RIGHTS RESERVED

EDITION PETERS

London · Frankfurt/M. · Leipzig · New York

Air from Suite No. 3 in D
'Air on the G string'